FAITH FOR AN UPSIDE-DOWN WORLD

ASCENSION to PENTECOST

A Devotional Inspired by Nature: Volume 5

Shirley D. Andrews

WestBow Press books may be ordered through booksellers or by contacting:

WestBow Press
A Division of Thomas Nelson & Zondervan
1663 Liberty Drive
Bloomington, IN 47403
www.westbowpress.com
844-714-3454

ISBN: 978-1-6642-7885-1 (sc)
ISBN: 978-1-6642-7886-8 (e)

Library of Congress Control Number: 2022917686

Print information available on the last page.

WestBow Press rev. date: 04/28/2023

CONTENTS

ACKNOWLEDGMENTS

I offer a special thank you to those who have lifted this project to God in prayer and have continually given me words of encouragement. Your prayers and support were essential in taking this devotional from vision to reality. I am especially appreciate of:

J. Michael Fuller, photographer extraordinaire and praying friend, whose photography inspired my writing in each part of "FAITH" – Ascencion to Pentecost: A Devotional Inspired by Nature Volume 5.

Johanna Calabro and Sharyl Backus, loving friends and intercessors, for their prayers and encouragement along this journey of faith, especially their prayers.

Matt Richmond, a servant of Jesus Christ, marketing services for this new project.

Rev. Jay Richmond, President of Renewal Prayer Network, member of Capital District Ministers Association, Albany, NY. Pastor Jay is a life-long friend who is making time to help me with media advertising and I am so grateful to him.

And a special thank you to those whose endorsements have blessed me and encouraged me to keep moving forward in a writing ministry for the purpose of making disciples for the transformation of the world:

Dr. Thomas F. Reid, retired pastor and author of several books.

Rev. Patricia Molik, Elder in the Upper New York Annual Conference, United Methodist Church.

Rev. Penny Brink, Elder in the Upper New York and Annual Conference, United Methodist Church.

Shirley D. Andrews

John 10: 9-10

PART 1

ASCENSION OF THE KING OF LOVE

The Resurrected Messiah, Jesus Christ, on the Road to Emmaus

"When they, the women, came back from the tomb, they told all these things to the Eleven and to all the others. It was Mary Magdalene, Joanna, Mary, the mother of James and the others with them who told this to the apostles. But they did not believe the women, because their words seemed to them like nonsense. Peter, however, got up and ran to the tomb. Bending over, he saw the strips of linen lying by themselves, and he went away, wondering to himself what had happened."

"Now that same day two of them were going to a village called Emmaus, about seven miles from Jerusalem. They were talking to each other about everything that had happened. As they talked and discussed these things with each other, Jesus himself came along and walked along with them; but they were kept from recognizing him."

"He asked them, 'What are you discussing together as you walk along?' They stood still; their faces downcast. One of them, named Cleopas, asked him, 'Are you only a visitor to Jerusalem and do not know the things that have happened there in these days? 'What things?' he asked. 'About Jesus of Nazareth,' they replied. 'He was a prophet, powerful in word and deed before God and all the people. The chief priests and our rulers handed him over to be sentenced to death, and they crucified him; but we had hoped that he was the one who was going to redeem Israel. And what is more, it is the third day since all this took place. In addition, some of our women amazed us. They went to the tomb early this morning but didn't find his body. They came and told us that they had seen a vision of angels, who said he was alive. Then some of our companions went to the tomb and found it just as the women had said, but him they did not see.'"

"He said to them, 'How foolish you are, and how slow of heart to believe all that the prophets have spoken! Did not the Christ have to suffer these things and then enter his glory?' And beginning with Moses and all the Prophets, he explained to them what was said in all the Scriptures concerning himself."

Luke 24: 9 – 27

"When he was at the table with them, he took bread, gave thanks, broke it, and began to give it to them. Then their eyes were opened and they recognized him, and he disappeared from their sight. They asked each other, 'Were not our hearts burning within us while he talked with us on the road and opened the Scriptures to us?'"

Luke 24: 30 – 32

Jesus Christ, The Risen Lord, Appears to the Disciples

"While they were still talking about this, Jesus himself stood among them and said to them, 'Peace be with you.'"

"They were startled and frightened, thinking they saw a ghost. He said to them, 'Why are you troubled and why do doubts rise in your minds? Look at my hands and my feet. It is I myself! Touch me and see; a ghost does not have flesh and bones, as you see I have.'"

"When he had said this he showed them his hands and feet. And while they still did not believe it because of joy and amazement, he asked them, 'Do you have anything here to eat?' They gave him a piece of broiled fish, and he took it and ate it in their presence."

"He said to them, 'This is what I told you while I was still with you: Everything must be fulfilled that is written about me in the Law of Moses, the Prophets and the Psalms.'"

"Then he opened their minds so they could understand the Scriptures. He told them, 'This is what is written: The Christ will suffer and rise from the dead on the third day, and repentance and forgiveness of sins will be preached in his name to all nations, beginning at Jerusalem. You are witnesses of these things. I am going to send you what my father has promised; but stay in the city until you have been clothed with power from on high.'"

Luke 24: 36 - 49

The Ascension of Jesus Christ, Our Risen Savior and Lord

"When he had led them out to the vicinity of Bethany, he lifted up his hands and blessed them. While he was blessing them, he left them and was taken up into heaven. Then they worshiped him and returned to Jerusalem with great joy. And they stayed continually at the temple, praising God."

Luke 24: 50 – 53

God's Testimony from the Old Testament written by the Prophet Isaiah

"' You are my witnesses,' declares the Lord, 'and my servant whom I have chosen, so that you may know and believe me and understand that I am he. Before me no god was formed nor will there be one after me. I, even I, am the Lord, and apart from me there is no Savior.

I have revealed, and saved and proclaimed – I, and not some foreign god among you. You are my witnesses,' declares the Lord, 'that I am God. Yes, and from ancient days I am he. No one can deliver out of my hand. When I act, who can reverse it?'"

Isaiah 43: 10 – 13

Faith of Our Fathers

1. Faith of our fa - thers! li - ving still In spite of dun - geon,
2. Faith of our fa - thers! we___ will strive To win all na - tions
3. Faith of our fa - thers! we___ will love Both friend and foe in

fire,___ and sword, O how our hearts___ beat high___ with joy
un - to thee, And thro' the truth___ that comes___ from God,
all___ our strife, And preach thee, too,___ as love___ knows how,

When - e'er we hear that glo - rious word! Faith of our fa - thers,
Man - kind shall then be tru - ly free: Faith of our fa - thers,
By kind - ly words and vir - tuous life; Faith of our fa - thers,

ho - ly faith! We will be true to thee till death!
ho - ly faith! We will be true to thee till death!
ho - ly faith! We will be true to thee till death!

Text: Frederick W. Faber, 1814-1863
Tune: Henry F. Hemy, 1818-1888;
last 8 measures, James G. Walton, 1821-1905

88 88 88
ST. CATHERINE
www.hymnary.org/text/faith_of_our_fathers_living_still

My Faith Looks Up to Thee

1 My faith looks up to thee, thou Lamb of Cal - va - ry,
2 May thy rich grace im - part strength to my fain - ting heart,
3 While life's dark maze I tread, and griefs a - round me spread,
4 When ends life's tran - sient dream, when death's cold, sul - len stream,

Sa - vior di - vine! Now hear me while I pray, take all my
my zeal in - spire; as thou hast died for me, O may my
be thou my guide; bid dark - ness turn to day, wipe sor - row's
shall o'er me roll; blest Sa - vior, then, in love fear and dis -

guilt a - way; O let me from this day be whol - ly thine!
love to thee pure, warm, and change - less be, a liv - ing fire!
tears a - way, nor let me e - ver stray from thee a - side.
trust re - move; O bear me safe a - bove, a ran - somed soul!

Text: Ray Palmer (1808-1887)
Tune: Lowell Mason (1792-1872)

664 66 64
OLIVET
www.hymnary.org/text/my_faith_looks_up_to_thee

Boreal Bob is known for his beautiful brown cap, black eye, plump tummy, long tail and white breast. These tiny birds are hard to find unless you travel to Canada or Alaska year around. His boreal habits and sedentary lifestyle is why he survives in one territory, the boreal region, cold with snow all year. They travel in small groups, sometimes with other songbirds such as kinglets. In summer and fall they hide seeds and insects to help them get through the long and brutal winter. Hiding food is known as "cashing."

In Canada, the Boreal "brown-capped" chickadee is not afraid of people and people love to feed them. Canadians have given these sweet songbirds folk names; two of these names are "Fillady" and "Chick Chick." The oldest recorded Boreal chickadee was at least five years and four months old when it was recaptured and released during a banding operation in Nova Scotia.

"In the past God spoke to our forefathers through the prophets at many times and in many ways, but in these last days he has spoken to us by his Son, whom he appointed heir of all things, and through whom he made the universe. The Son is the radiance of God's glory and the exact representation of his being, sustaining all things by his powerful word. After he had provided purification for sins, he sat down at the right hand of the Majesty in heaven."
Hebrews 1: 1-3

Did God create this beautiful Boreal chickadee? According to this scripture, not only is God's word "Truth" but his word and his Son, Jesus, also called the "Truth" is creating and sustaining all kinds of chickadees, 105 species of sparrows, so many different owls, people from all different languages all over the world, the mountains and the seas are his creation, not to mention all the different kinds of fish in the oceans. Yes, he, Jesus is not only creator of all living things but he is sustaining all things with his powerful word, the Bible. You may remember that he said, **"I am the Way, the Truth and the Life, no one comes to the Father except by Me."**
John 14: 6.

Prayer: Lord God, Creator of all living things and sustainer of all life on earth, it is hard to believe, that as the war in the Ukraine rages on and so many people are dying because of the Russian invasion, that justice will prevail. Then I look back at John 14:6 above and know in my heart that many who have died in the war were saved and are with you now in heaven. They had a loving relationship with you before the war and had already asked for forgiveness for their sin by accepting your blood shed on the Cross at Calvary. Remind me every day to continue to pray for lost souls so even those who are reading this page today will be sure to get right with You, God, by confessing their sin, receiving your love into their hearts, and now are saved by faith in Jesus and what He did on the Cross, in Jesus' powerful name, Amen.

PURPLE FINCH – *male enjoying the attention*   *Carpodacus purpureus*

Duanesburg, New York   *Uncommon*

....

The color of the Purple finch is really not purple but a rather old rose color. The Purple finch is the bird that Roger Tory Peterson famously described as a "sparrow dipped in raspberry juice." They are great singers. In their rich warbling songs, Purple finches sometimes add in the sounds of other species, including Barn swallows, American Gold finches, Eastern Towhee and Brown – headed cowbirds. What fun to be deep in the woods when this amazing Songbird choir starts their choir rehearsal and we are invited to listen. We will give God a handclap of praise for his concert in nature and we were invited! Tickets for this concert are always free.

In courtship, the male hops near the female with his wings drooping, tail raised, chest puffed out, then vibrates his wings until he rises a short distance in the air. He may be holding bits of nest material in his bill and sing a soft song in this performance. Both parents feed the 3 -6 young finches with seeds and insects found in trees and shrubs. At birth, the finch babies are naked, eyes closed and helpless. There are 17 North American species of finches and 234 species of finches in the whole world. The life span of the Purple finch is 3-4 years with many reaching 6-7 years.

"But I will sing of your strength, in the morning I will sing of your love; for you are my fortress, my refuge in times of trouble. You are my strength, I sing praise to you, you God, are my fortress, my God on whom I rely."
Psalm 59: 16-17

Roger Tory Peterson, mentioned in the first paragraph, is famous for his findings and writings about birds. His PETERSON FIELD GUIDE TO BIRDS of Eastern and Central North America has wonderful information about many, many species of birds. He calls the Purple finch a "Sparrow dipped in raspberry juice;" as creative as you can get and is the greatest way to remember that the Purple finch is not purple. Every spring the Purple finches join the "Woodland" choir along with all those singing birds mentioned in the first paragraph. Their beautiful singing is their way of giving God, their Creator, measures and measures of loving praise. God, our Creator, wanted the woods to be filled with songs of praise for Him and His love shown at the Cross of Calvary, not only for you and me, but for all who He gave ears to hear. The Cross of Christ is for all sinners who accept Jesus as Lord and Savior. He paid our sin debt in full by His blood shed for us. Let's give God praise just like the birds do when they sing.

Prayer: Lord God, Creator of all life in the whole world, we offer up our praise this day and say thank you for every bird in the forest and every animal on earth. Lord, we need to be drawing closer and closer to you as each day comes and goes. We are living in dangerous and perilous times with so much hate and we know that you and what you did on the Cross is the only kind of love that can change hearts from evil to eternal love in heaven with you. Thank you for your blood that will never lose its power, in Jesus' name, Amen.

SANDHILL CRANES – *sharing a spectacular sunset*   Grus canandensis

New Mexico   Common

Whether stepping singly and slowly across a wet meadow or filling the sky by the hundreds and thousands, Sandhill cranes have an elegance that draws attention. These tall, gray-bodied, crimson-capped, long-legged birds breed in open wetlands, fields and prairies across North America. They group together in great numbers, filling the air with distinctive rolling cries that can be heard from miles around.

Mates display to each other with exuberant dances that retain a gangly grace. Sandhill crane populations are generally strong, but isolated populations in Mississippi and Cuba are endangered. Their bugling calls are unique and your eyes will look skyward in anticipation of a very large display of their wide wingspan; their noisy call can help alert you to this species presence, particularly as they pass overhead on migration. Their wing span is six to seven feet wide and very impressive when in flight.

"Yet this I call to mind and therefore I have hope: Because of the Lord's great love we are not consumed, for his compassions never fail. They are new every morning; great is your faithfulness. I say to myself, 'The Lord is my portion; therefore, I will wait for him. The Lord is good to those whose hope is in him, it is good to wait quietly for the salvation of the Lord.'"
Lamentations 3: 21-26

This photo of two cranes in silhouette surrounded by a powerfully intense sunset is spectacular. To say it is inspiring and reflective of more than just daylight or darkness is true. Two matched birds in size, in position, at sunset, standing still for the camera and silent as if mesmerized by the beauty around them. If it were said that this photo and others like it are created to focus on the beauty in God's world of wild things and to bring God glory, would you agree? Could God be reminding you that his love for you is like a beautiful and colorful photo of the faithfulness of God and the hope you have in him? Have you waited quietly and received the salvation God gives? Answer these questions honestly and then join in the following prayer.

Prayer: Lord God, my Faithful Father, Son and Holy Spirit, who has great love for me, thank you for your great love for Sandhill cranes and for all of your creation; You are the Lord who died for me and rose again from the grave to give me life eternal in heaven. I take great delight in photos like this that speak so personally to me about your love and faithfulness. Knowing that your compassions never fail and are new every morning is an awesome blessing. Even though I do not like waiting, my hope is in you and I will wait until I hear your voice each new day. Speak, Lord, your child is listening, in Jesus' name, Amen.

Young Downy Pied-billed Grebe's sport zebra-like stripes in great contrast to their grebe parents. They are small, chunky, swimming birds with thick bills that turn silver. They are part bird and part submarine. The Pied-billed grebe is far less sociable than most grebes, almost never in flocks. Often can be found alone on small marshy ponds. They can fly but rarely are seen in flight. They feed by diving from the surface and swimming underwater. Their feet paddle away under their body to propel through the water.

The photo on the next page is this same grebe, you can call hm "Greg Grebe," with new facts about his life on these small ponds. These grebes migrate mostly at night in late fall and early spring. That fact is also true of the young Atlantic Puffin who leaves the nest for the first time at night as well. The Puffins fly out to sea alone and never come back home.

Like other Grebes, Pied-billed Grebe's eat large quantities of their own feathers. Feathers may at times fill up more than half a Grebe's stomach, and feathers are sometimes fed to newly hatched chicks. Among other reasons, this helps form indigestible items into pellets which they can regurgitate.

"If we live, we live for the Lord; and if we die, we die for the Lord. So, whether we live or die, we belong to the Lord."

Romans 14: 8

God is the Creator of all the people in this world; Creator of all animals, birds, water fowl and all living things. He created beautiful flowers and trees, fields of tomatoes and peppers, wheat and corn fields, oceans and mountains, waterfalls; sunsets, hot sun and cold rain and snow and so much more. This scripture tells us that Christians, God lovers, belong to God. Every breath comes from him and he takes breath away when we die. He loves his children and has provided so much beauty in creation for us to enjoy. The Grebes are interesting water fowl and like us humans they can get frightened and want to disappear. God loves them so much he made a way for them to disappear when they are afraid. If he takes such good care of Grebes how much more will he take care of you, his child!

Prayer: Lord God, thank you for loving me and all the creatures you have created. I love the Grebes, they are fun to learn about and then to also remember all the other beautiful parts of creation that we, your children, get to enjoy. It is really quite simple, You protect my life every day just as you do with the water fowl, song birds and all the beautiful flowers. If we live, we live for you, if we die, we die for you. You are the center of my life and I am so grateful to know this great love you have for all you have created. It is a wonderful feeling to belong to the Lord, Creator of the whole wide world, in Jesus' name, Amen.

Greg grebe is back to show off for you so you will remember more about how he lives and survives in the wilderness. During breeding season, they like to hide from the rest of the world. They are secretive and will hide in places hard to find. Besides hiding, they like to sing or maybe that's the wrong word! Actually, they make bizarre whinnying, gobbling, cooing noises by day or night.

Grebes like very quiet places to hang out but that is not always possible. After all, they are sharing this pond in the wilderness with many other creatures. They love quiet days and nights but when there is a loud disturbance, they are very frightened and scared. So, Gregg grebe is showing us how he disappears when he is afraid. Notice that he is disappearing under the water, starting with the middle of his body, down, down, down, until he has disappeared. Please remember that God made him that way because God loves him and wants to protect him from being harmed. Once under the water, he will swim far away from the noise and disturbance on the other side of the pond.

"For God so loved the world that he gave his one and only Son that whosoever believes in him shall not perish but have eternal life. For God did not send his Son into the world to condemn the world, but to save the world through him."

John 3: 16 - 17

If God loves his grebes so much and protects them from fearful noises, how much more does he love you because you are made in God's image? God's love for you is unmeasurable and it is free forever if you will believe that the Son of God (JESUS) died for you on a cross a long time ago and rose from the dead. We celebrate his Resurrection from the grave on Easter. If you believe, you will live with Jesus in heaven someday. Our Father in heaven sent Jesus, His Son, to die for our sin so whosoever will can become a child of God and live for him on earth now and later to live in heaven with him forever.

Prayer: Lord God, Thank you for your Son, Jesus, who has saved me from sin and death when he went to the cross on the first Good Friday and then rose from the grave to give me eternal life with him in heaven. You were not angry with me but you poured out your compassion and unconditional love so I might become a new creation in Christ. I will never be able to repay you for such a gift as salvation. I will spend eternity giving thanks and glory to you every day. Thank you for the grebes who are beautiful creatures who love quiet places and live a peaceful life if they are left to themselves with no scary noises or sudden interruptions. I am glad that you made them to disappear when they are afraid. The Bible says that you will never leave me or forsake me, how do I thank such a loving God? No words today, just a very happy heart, in Jesus' name, Amen.

The Brown-headed cowbird is a stocky blackbird with an amazing approach to raising his children. Females forgo building nests and instead put all their energy into producing eggs, sometimes more than three dozen in one summer. Now, here is a twist to this story – they lay the eggs in nests of other birds. This usually means that some species of vireo or maybe some species of warbler are now foster parents to the cowbirds. Can't you just hear Charlie Brown saying, "good grief!" This often not only irritates the warblers but they may get pushed out of the nest before they are ready to leave home. This will not surprise you either, "nuisance bird" becomes the cowbirds new identity! The fact is: because of this behavior, they have caused the decline in the Kirtland's warbler and the Black-capped vireo families. "Nuisance" means that the cowbirds destroy the eggs of the vireo and even will destroy new baby warblers by pushing them out of the nest.

"Let no debt remain outstanding, except the continuing debt to love one another, for he who loves his fellowman has fulfilled the law. The commandments, 'Do not commit adultery, Do not murder, Do not steal, Do not covet, and any other commandment there may be, are summed up in this rule: Love your neighbor as yourself. Love does no harm to its neighbor. Therefore, love is the fulfillment of the law.'"

Romans 13: 8-10

Sin is the issue for all who read these scriptures. The cowbird is just one example of the evil intensions of not only some birds but all human life is born in original sin and we all need a Savior. It is our heart condition that needs to be changed and surrendered to Jesus, God's only Son. Jesus was born sinless, of a virgin, on the first Christmas. This same, sinless, forgiving Jesus died on the "Old Rugged Cross" at Calvary. Hymn books are full of precious songs about Jesus and what he did for us on the Cross; some are included in this book and in the other four Devotionals already published and available on the internet. www.shirleydandrews.com

The Holy Bible proclaims the commandments that are listed above and Calvary's place where Jesus was crucified, also everything that happened before Jesus was born in the flesh until he was pierced for our transgressions. When he bled to death, the bright sky went black for 3 hours. On the third day he rose from the grave. He is waiting in heaven for you.

Prayer: Lord God, I know in my heart that I need to be saved. You are the only Savior. Save me, Lord, I am a sinner and need your forgiveness. I surrender all and I desire a personal relationship with you, Jesus, or I know I will perish in my sin, with my destiny in hell. I realize that the world, the flesh, (pride) and the devil are my enemies and I ask for your mercy and grace to trade all sin, pride and selfish desires for Praise and Thanksgiving for you, Lord, the one True and Holy God. Thank you, Jesus, for the Cross that makes all of this possible. The old has past, the new is here, I am a new creation in Christ because he first loved me and now I will always pray in Jesus' name with a grateful heart, Amen.

Adult Bald eagles are at least four to five years old with white heads and white tails. Juveniles are less than four years of age and have not yet developed a white head and tail. Eagles are predators, birds of prey and take their food by attacking and over-powering smaller birds, fish or any smaller animal.

At the National Eagle Center in Wabasha, Minnesota, they record eagle siting every week at eight different locations near Wabasha. The week of March 25, 2022 they recorded 121 adult and young total. If you love eagles, you can visit their Eagle-watch Cam on the Internet.

It is very exciting when in the presence of an adult Bald eagle. The largest wing-span of an adult American Bald eagle has been recorded at 8.2 feet. This eagle lives in Kachemak Bay, Alaska.

"Does the eagle soar at your command and build his nest on high? He dwells on a cliff and stays there at night; a rocky crag is his stronghold. From there he seeks out his food; his eyes detect it from afar. His young one's feast on blood, and where the slain are, there is he."
Job 39: 27 – 30

Job has a trying life; very complicated, full of sorrow and grief and so many attacks by the enemy of man. As you know, Satan, our enemy, has many other names to describe his goal of destruction in the lives of believers. In this scripture, Job is questioning God about his creation, especially the eagle. He asks if God helps the eagle make decisions and live high, close to God or in a privileged place chosen by God? It is as if he is envious of the eagle because the eagle's life seems so uncomplicated. He reminds God that the Eagle Eye is a great attribute for finding food for the family. Also, the eagle has a safe place, his own cliff, the eagle seems to stand strong no matter what is going on in his life. Job has an encounter with our Lord and Godly wisdom flows so if you have time read Job: 42, the last chapter and experience the amazing grace of our Lord.

Prayer: Lord God, my faithful, loving Savior, You provided me with everything needed to live a victorious life over sin and death. The Cross of Calvary was anything but easy! It was so painful, so much more horrible than anything that Job experienced and you obeyed our Heavenly Father and shed your blood to set me free; Sinless blood shed for sinful mankind. Your resurrection from the dead is the gift of eternal life in heaven for all believers who place their faith in you and the cross. No one is worthy of this mercy and grace. Only You, Jesus, are worthy and I give you all my praise and especially my gratitude for my salvation that makes all the rest of life possible, in Jesus' name, the name above all name, Amen.

Breath-taking red all year around, cardinals do not migrate and they do not molt into dull plumage. They are especially stunning in winter on snow. They can take your breath away anytime, anywhere. In summer, their sweet whistles are one of the first sounds of the morning. "Carl Cardinal" is patiently waiting for his best friend, Carrie. Carl and Carrie mate for life after he notices that Carrie is the best female cardinal he has ever seen! To say that they "fall in love" is very true in the bird world as God planned it that way when he created cardinals. Some people say that 'when cardinals appear, angels are near.'"

Only a few female North American songbirds sing. North American female cardinals do sing and often while they are sitting on the eggs in the nest. A mated pair of cardinals share song phrases, but the female may sing a longer and slightly more complex song than the male.

The male cardinal fiercely defends its breeding territory from the other males. When a male sees its reflection in glass surfaces, it frequently will spend hours fighting the imaginary intruder. When you turn to page 23 you will read about "Messengers from Heaven" from a folklore source.

"For since the creation of the world God's invisible qualities – his eternal power and divine nature – have been clearly seen, being understood from what has been made, so that people are without excuse. For although they knew God, they neither glorified him as God nor gave thanks to him, but their thinking became futile and their foolish hearts were darkened."
Romans 1: 20 – 21

What happens to you, when out for a walk, you see a male cardinal? Do you think, like some folks, "when cardinals appear, angels are near?" Maybe you know that if you stand very still, his female life-long mate may be moving near as well. Perhaps you are reminded that God, our Heavenly Father, created these gorgeous solid red song birds. Now you want to give thanks to God for the beauty all around you today, especially for cardinals. It is God's eternal power and divine nature that cause our hearts to respond to what he and only he has made for the world's enjoyment. Let's pray boldly for more cardinals in our life and for protection from a foolish heart that can become dark. Next time you see a cardinal, stop, and let God's love fill you. God has created many cardinals but there is only one of you and his love for you is beyond measure.

Prayer: Lord God, your cardinals take my breath away and I just want to sing loud praises to you when I see them. Please bless me and all our readers with many cardinal visits when we least expect them! Surely it will take my breath away again and again. Next time a cardinal appears, I will open my heart to receive your love and always give thanks for your eternal power and divine nature, in Jesus' name and for his sake, Amen.

To God Be the Glory

Text: Fanny J. Crosby, 1875, alt.
Tune: William H. Doane, 1875

11 11 11 11 with refrain
TO GOD BE THE GLORY
www.hymnary.org/text/to_god_be_the_glory_great_things_he_hath

Lord, praise the Lord; let the peo - ple re - joice! O come to the

Fa -ther through Je -sus the Son, and give him the glo - ry; great things he has done.

THE GREAT COMMISSION

"Then the eleven Disciples went to Galilee, to the mountain that Jesus had told them to go. When they saw him, they worshiped him; but some doubted. Then Jesus came to them and said, 'All authority in heaven and on earth has been given me. Therefore, go and make disciples of all nations, baptizing them in the name of the Father and of the Son and of the Holy Spirit, and teaching them to obey everything I have commanded you. And surely I am with you always, to they very end of the age.'"

Matthew 28:16-20

"Messengers from Heaven"

Cardinals are among the most treasured gifts that nature shares with us during our time on earth. But this beautiful songbird's reach goes far beyond our physical world. Long associated with Heaven and the promise of the spiritual realm, Cardinals are widely believed to be messengers from above, the embodiment of loved ones who have gone before us. Now, the symbolism of the Cardinal and the comfort it brings in times of loss are celebrated in photos, jewelry, tree ornaments and paintings by famous artists.

The cardinal bird and its theological virtues are found in the Vatican Museums in Vatican City.

Saved by FAITH and Not by Works

"For God so loved the world that he gave his one and only Son, that whoever believes in him shall not perish but have eternal life. For God did not send his Son into the world to condemn the world, but to save the world through him. Whoever believes in him is not condemned, but whoever does not believe stands condemned already because he has not believed in the name of God's one and only Son. This is the verdict: Light has come into the world, but men loved darkness instead of light because their deeds were evil. Everyone who does evil hates the light, and will not come into the light for fear that his deeds will be exposed.

But whoever lives by the truth comes into the light, so that it may be seen plainly that what he has done has been done through God."

John 3: 15-21

CHOOSE WISELY, CHOOSE CHRIST and HIM CRUCIFIED

Faith in God is always free; free as a warm and refreshing ocean breeze,

Faith goes very deep; so much deeper than the roots of old Redwood trees.

Faith travels with you, wherever you go, as far as the east is from the west;

Faith praises God, whether in a difficult trial or need of some rest.

Faith in Jesus saves whosoever will; His eternal love in your heart is His goal;

Faith brings daily peace and joy; prayer and praise from deep in your soul.

Faith in God's sinless blood shed on the Cross, is saving you, covering your sin;

Faith in Jesus Christ, from your beginning to its end, brings you an eternal win!

Faith for this day, you are never promised more, what is this precious day for?

Faith to love and draw closer to God, social media rush? Better golf score?

Faith blesses all who choose Jesus; He will never twist anyone's arm;

Faith never stops loving you, leading you or protecting you from Satan's harm.

Faith forever; joining God in heaven when life is over, your breath is no more;

Faith as small as a mustard seed He allows; receive God's love today and soar!

Choose wisely, my friend, and all who read " FAITH: Ascension to Pentecost."

By Shirley D. Andrews - 2022

PART 2
PENTECOST
The King of Love Sends to Earth "Tongues of Fire!"

"When the day of Pentecost came, they were all together in one place. Suddenly a sound like the blowing of a violent wind came from heaven and filled the whole house where they were sitting. They saw what seemed to be "tongues of fire" that separated and came to rest on each of them. All of them were filled with the Holy Spirit and began to speak in other tongues as the Spirit enabled them."

"Now there were staying in Jerusalem God-fearing Jews from every nation under heaven. When they heard this sound, a crowd came together in bewilderment, because each one heard them speaking in his own language. Utterly amazed, they asked, 'Are not all these men who are speaking Galileans? Then how is it that each of us hears them in his own native language? (verses 9-11 list 16 different languages that were detected as the Holy Spirit filled and spoke through these people). 'We hear them declaring the wonders of God in our own tongues!' Amazed and perplexed, they asked one another, 'What does this mean?'"

"Some, however, made fun of them and said, 'they have had too much wine.'"

"Then Peter stood up with the Eleven, raised his voice and addressed the crowd: 'Fellow Jews and all of you who live in Jerusalem, let me explain this to you; listen carefully to what I say. These men are not drunk, as you suppose. It's only nine in the morning! No, this is what was spoken by the prophet Joel!'"

"In the last days, God says, 'I will pour out my Spirit on all peoples. Your sons and daughters will prophesy, your young men will see visions, your old men will dream dreams. Even on my servants, both men and women, I will pour out my Spirit in those days, and they will prophesy. I will show wonders in the heavens above and signs on the earth below, blood and fire and billows of smoke. The sun will be turned to darkness and the moon to blood before the coming of the great and glorious day of the Lord. And everyone who calls on the name of the Lord will be saved.'"

"Men of Israel, listen to this: Jesus of Nazareth was a man accredited by God to you by miracles, wonders and signs, which God did among you through him, as you yourselves know. This man was handed over to you by God's set purpose and foreknowledge; and you, with the help of wicked men, put him to death by nailing him to the cross. But God raised him from the dead, freeing him from the agony of death, because it was impossible for death to keep its hold on him. David said about him: 'I saw the Lord always before me. Because he is always at my right hand, I will not be shaken. Therefore, my heart is glad and my tongue rejoices; my body will also live in hope, because you will not abandon me to the grave, nor will you let your Holy

One see decay. You have made known to me the path of life; you will fill me with joy in your presence. Brothers, I will tell you confidently that the patriarch David died and was buried and the tomb is here to this day. But he was a prophet and knew that God has promised him an oath that he would place one of his descendants on his throne. Seeing what was ahead, he spoke of the resurrection of the Christ, that he was not abandoned to the grave, nor did his body see decay. God has raised this Jesus to life, and we are all witnesses of the fact. Exalted to the right hand of God, he has received from the Father the promised Holy Spirit and has poured out what you see and hear. For David did not ascend to heaven, and yet he said, 'The Lord has said to my Lord: Sit at my right hand until I make your enemies a footstool for your feet.'"

"Therefore, let all Israel be assured of this: God has made this Jesus, whom you crucified, both Lord and Christ."

"When the people heard this, they were cut to the heart and said to Peter and the other apostles, 'Brothers, what shall we do?'"

"Peter replied, 'Repent and be baptized, every one of you, in the name of Jesus Christ for the forgiveness of your sins. And you will receive the gift of the Holy Spirit. The promise is for you and your children and to all who are far off – for all whom the Lord our God will call.'"

"With many other words he warned them; and he pleaded with them; 'Save yourselves from this corrupt generation.' Those who accepted his message were baptized, and about three thousand were added to their number that day." They devoted themselves to the apostles teaching and to the fellowship, to the breaking of bread and to prayer. Everyone was filled with awe, and many wonders and miraculous signs were done by

John and Peter Begin Healing Prayer, in the Name of Jesus Christ of Nazareth, through the Power of the Holy Spirit.

"When he saw Peter and John about to enter, he asked them for money. Peter said, 'Silver and gold I do not have, but what I have I give you. In the name of Jesus Christ of Nazareth, walk.' Taking him by the right hand, he helped him up, and instantly the man's feet and ankles became strong. He jumped to his feet and began to walk. Then he went with them into the temple courts, walking and jumping, and praising God." Acts 3: 3-8

---

the apostles. All the believers were together and had everything in common. Selling their possessions and goods, they gave to anyone as he had need. Every day they continued to meet together in the temple courts. They broke bread in their homes and ate together with glad and sincere hearts, praising God and enjoying the favor of all the people. And the Lord added to their number daily those who were being saved." Excerpts from **Acts 2: 1 – 47**

NAMES FOR THE HOLY SPIRIT

BREATH OF THE ALMIGHTY	Job 33:4	The Holy Spirit is the life-giving breath of God.
COUNSELOR and COMFORTER	John 14:16, 26;	The Holy Spirit comforts, counsels and gives strength.
ETERNAL SPIRIT	Hebrews 9:14	The Holy Spirit is Eternal God.
FREE SPIRIT	Psalm 51:12	The Holy Spirit is God's free, generous and willing Spirit.
GOD	Acts 5:3-4	The Holy Spirit is the Third Person of the Trinity.
SPIRIT OF TRUTH	John 14:16	The Father gives a Counselor, the Spirit of Truth to be with you forever.
HOLY SPIRIT	Psalm 51:11	God is Spirit and that Spirit is Holy. He is the Spirit of Holiness.
LORD	2Cor. 3:16-17	Like Jesus and the Father, the Holy Spirit is also addressed and worshiped as LORD.
POWER OF THE HIGHEST	Luke 1:35	The Spirit is God's power, the Greatest power there is.
SPIRIT OF MIGHT	Isaiah 4:4	The Holy Spirit is the Spirit of Strength.
SPIRIT OF ADOPTION	Romans 8:15	He is the Spirit by which we are made God's children.
SPIRIT OF BURNING	Isaiah 4:4	The Spirit is God's fire of purification.
SPIRIT OF JUDGEMENT	Isaiah 4:4; 28:6	The Spirit of God brings conviction and judgement.
SPIRIT OF CHRIST	Romans 8:9	The Holy Spirit is Jesus' own Spirit.
SPIRIT OF GLORY	1 Peter 4:14	The Spirit always gives glory to Christ.

HOLY SPIRIT OF FAITH

Words and Music by Shirley D. Andrews

REFRAIN:

Holy Spirit of Truth set me free; let me dance, be all I can be;
Holy Spirit of Fire burn in me; Refiner's fire for all to see;
Holy Spirit of Life breathe through me the breath of the Almighty;
Holy Spirit of Faith grow great in me; glorify the Trinity!

Verse 1. God's Spirit is moving across all this land. He's claiming each heart that will take His hand. Don't miss the chance to worship with Him, Just ask His Spirit to fill from within.

REFRAIN:

Verse 2. The end times are nearing, has your heart grown cold? The warnings are here, is your passion still bold? Turn back and ask Him to renew your heart; He will give you another start.

REFRAIN:

Verse 3. The choices are two, it is heaven or hell; The Spirit is calling and wants us to tell that Christ is the Bridegroom, He's calling His bride. Prepare your heart, stay close to His side!

REFRAIN:

> *"Sing to the Lord a new song; sing to the Lord, all the earth. Sing to the Lord, praise his name; proclaim his salvation day after day. Declare his glory among the nations, his marvelous deeds among all the peoples. For great is the Lord and most worthy of praise; he is to be feared above all gods. For all the gods of the nations are idols, but the Lord made the heavens. Splendor and majesty are before him; strength and glory are In his sanctuary." Psalm 96:1-6*

God does not listen to our singing voice or our speaking voice. God listens to our heart. He loves our speaking and singing heart. To him we are making a joyful noise, whether speaking or singing His praises. The heartfelt sound is delivered to Him from **our heart of faith.** We praise Him for His pleasure because of who He is. Why do we love Him and praise His name from deep down in our heart? Because all the power that we need to live a victorious life in obedience to His word is found in His blood poured out on Calvary's Cross for the forgiveness of the sins of the world. Sinless God, Jesus Christ, fully man and fully God, first loved us, sinful mankind, and then laid His life down and died for us! **"But the Lord said to Samuel, 'do not consider his appearance or his height, for I have rejected him. The Lord does not look at the things people look at. People look at the outward appearance, but the Lord looks at the heart.'"**
1 Samuel 16 -17

This male yellow-headed blackbird has just found a tasty morsel to ward off hunger for a while. He has landed on two cattails that are some distance apart. Maybe he is just showing off for the camera. Anyway, he is beautifully dressed in yellow, black and white and he is showing us his great athleticism. One of his greatest traits is that he is very gregarious. He loves to be around his blackbird friends and their families. Should you happen to find a large flock of red-winged blackbirds, focus on white wing patches and yellow heads; there very likely is one or more read-winged hanging out with their yellow-headed cousins.

Breaking News: He may attract up to eight females to nest within his area. No, he does not feed all those new babies. The female yellow-headed moms have to do that job. The oldest yellow-headed Blackbird on record was 11 years, 8 months old. This bird had been banded in Saskatchewan and was found in Nebraska.

"The end of all things is near. Therefore, be clear minded and self-controlled so that you can pray. Above all, love each other deeply, because love covers a multitude of sins. Offer hospitality to one another without grumbling."
1 Peter 4: 7- 9

The gregarious, loving and joyful yellow-headed blackbirds gather together in large groups because they love to be together. Even the cousins visit often and they do life together. Looks like a healthy Christian extended family or a Christian church that studies the Bible together, prays together, worships together and carries each other's burdens, doesn't it? Yes, we have a lot to learn about the Christian life from even the different kinds of blackbirds. God is our example of love and as human beings we can spend time with Jesus alone and together to help us grow in grace as the end of all things is near according to the Apostle Peter in this scripture. Let 's make the most of the time we have left on earth and ask God for Holy Spirit power to glorify Him and make us more like Jesus.

Prayer: Lord God, thank you for the example of the different kinds of blackbirds that get along so well, live together, travel together and truly love one another's company. We, as humans, have the same responsibility to love others because God's love is to be shared with everyone. The truth is, You God, first loved me, so I can love you and others. You displayed unconditional love for me on the Cross when you bled and died to save me from sin and death. God, You deserve all my attention and praise as I live in your presence and serve you with great joy! May the whole world come to know you and the peace that you give to all who believe, in Jesus' name and for His sake, Amen.

Meet "Nutty Red" who is an intense bundle of energy. Tiny and very active, you can find him in Northern woods and Western mountains. This long billed, short tailed songbird travels often with chickadees, kinglets and woodpeckers. Mom and Pop build their nest together to birth their new brood of babies. They collect resin from conifer trees. Pop puts the resin around the outside of the hole while Mom puts it inside of the hole. The resin can be a deterrent to invaders. The happy couple avoid the resin by diving swiftly in and out of this sticky hole.

Nuthatches often appear to be hyper-active especially when looking for their next meal or to feed their newborn nuthatches. These Nuthatches are fierce defenders of their nest before, during and after building them. They are aggressive, chasing away other hole-nesting birds such as the House wren, White-breasted nuthatches and Downy woodpeckers. A feisty nuthatch may go after much larger warblers, finches and swallows. You can find Red-breasted Nuthatches by listening for their nasal, yammering call or for the sound of a chickadee. They scoot up and down tree trunks at jerky rapid speed. You could say that when they are hungry they are hyper!

"And so, we know and rely on the love God has for us. God is love. Whoever lives in love lives in God, and God in them."

1 John 4: 16

The Nuthatch and his mate are very loving toward each other. How do we know that? They work together successfully. They are energetic and use this energy to build the perfect nest to raise their family. God created them that way. Why? Because God loves all the living things he has created. God's love for all life cannot be measured because his love never ends, it is eternal; and God has made a place called heaven for all life to live with him in peace forever!

Prayer: Lord God, your plan is so beautiful, so perfect, so exciting and so glorifying to you, Heavenly Father, Jesus, Son of God and the Holy Spirit, who lives in us. Thank you for the Cross of Calvary that made all this possible. Since I gave my heart to you, I have been growing in wisdom and knowledge of who you are, what you have done and how very, very much you love me and all of your creation. I am blessed beyond belief; so, I sing along daily with these beautiful birds and praise the Holy name of Jesus; I love you, Lord, forever and ever, Amen.

Aim your eyes high when looking for these orioles. They are most often seen perched at the tops of trees or flitting through the upper foliage in search of insects. Listen for their distinctive chatter, which is unlike the call of any other bird where orioles occur. Noisy nestlings may get your attention so follow the sound and you may find a nest very high off the ground. Northern Orioles seem to prefer only ripe, dark-colored fruit. They seek out the darkest mulberries, the reddest cherries and the deepest purple grapes, and will ignore green grapes and yellow cherries even if they are ripe. Their bright orange, white and really black feathers remind us of Halloween colors but you may never see a person dressed like an oriole for a Halloween parade. Females become deeper orange with every molt. Some older females are almost as bright orange as the males.

"When Jesus saw the crowd around him, he gave orders to cross to the other side. Then a teacher of the law came to him and said, 'Teacher, I will follow you where ever you go.' Jesus replied, 'Foxes have holes and the birds of the air have nests, but the Son of Man has no place to lay his head.'"
Matthew 8: 18 – 22

Jesus is Son of God and Son of Man. Jesus most often used the 'Son of Man' when talking about himself to others. In this scripture he is sharing the fact that He, God, Creator of all life has provided for every living thing that he created. Birds have nests, foxes have holes, but didn't Jesus have a big, beautiful house with all the luxuries to go home to after a full day of work? What do you mean, God? No bed to sleep in? That's right, dear children, someone who knew Jesus and loved him would invite him to their extra bed; That happened night after night. The Bible even tells us that he slept outside under the stars that he created. We hope it wasn't rainy nights! So, what does this scripture really say about Jesus? Yes, you are right; he wants us to know that even if we do not have a bed that we are not to worry because Jesus will take care of us. He endured the pain and agony of the Cross, shed his blood, to show us that if we believe in him and ask him for forgiveness for our sin, He will provide for our every need now and throughout eternity. We can never be too grateful for what Jesus has done for the human race he created. Let's give back to him our praise and thanksgiving prayers every day.

Prayer: Lord God, what you have done for us, sinners, who need your forgiveness is more than miraculous and so generous and filled with unconditional love, joy, and peace. We give you our highest praise as we lift Holy Hands toward heaven. Forgive me, Lord, when I go days without sending my praise heavenward to you. You are so worthy and I am not; remind me daily to be more and more grateful for the pain and agony of the Cross that has set me free from sin and death, in the precious name of Jesus, the name above all names, Amen.

An adult Black bear looking for more fun in the sun; or is he hungry? His running pace may say that he is famished or thirsty and knows just where to find whatever he needs. We will never know but let's learn more about one adult black bear so we can make an educated opinion about why he is running so fast.

Enjoy the next scripture and Ture Story that follows.

"I will never forget your precepts, for by them you have preserved my life."
Psalm 119: 93

A Devotional True Story – by Shirley D. Andrews

One morning after a very heavy snow fall, my Dad, who usually drove me to my first "one room School House" when I was 6 years old in 1st grade, could not get our car unburied. He went to the barn and rolled out a sleigh, bridled one of the horses in the barn and placed me in the passenger seat as he took the reins and sat in the driver's seat. What a ride, "Over the River and through the Woods" to school I flew. How did I stay warm on that amazing ride? Dad had pulled a huge Black bear fur blanket out of the barn and draped it on me and was I warm! That day has never left my memory and never will. That was only one of the many, many ways my Dad showed me the love of my Heavenly Father by being a faithful, loving Father here on earth!

The next year we moved to our first big house in Bristol Center, N.Y. While there, our family grew to 5 children. My sister, Bev and I, continued to be educated in another one room School that was bigger with 1st to 8th grade under one roof with no partitions. When 4th grade reading was called by the teacher, 4 of us walked up to the front of the room and took a seat on the long bench. Near the middle of 4th grade our school was closed and off we went on a big yellow bus to a school with many rooms under many roofs with lots of stairs.

Personal Prayer: Lord God, my Heavenly Father, thank you for choosing such wonderful, faithful parents for the DeSmith children. Thank you for sleigh rides and Black bear blankets, for how you are still protecting me in 2022. You are guiding us, Writer and Photographer, helping us to bring the truth of God's word to a lost world. Holy God, your love never fails. Your mercies are new every morning. I give you the highest praise from my heart today and so look forward to what your plan is for tomorrow, in Jesus' name, who went to the cross, bled and died for my sin and all sinners; who now can repent and turn back to a Holy, Loving and Saving God. Rejoice with me, Shirley, today as I give thanks for my life in Christ, my siblings, who also are being blessed with long life, for Jesus' sake, Amen.

This boldly patterned shorebird has lots of black and brown feathers and his head is all black feathers. Notice his long, orange chisel-shaped bill and piercing eye; take a look at his pink feet. They are not webbed but he is an excellent swimmer.

There are two different kinds of oystercatchers; the Black and the American Oystercatcher. The American looks different with a large white breast, dark blue head, black back feathers and the same eye and long orange bill like his cousin. "Ollie Oystercatcher" is standing on sandy ground surrounded by oyster shells. An oystercatcher doesn't "catch" oysters and mussels, but uses his bill to pry them open. Their process to open the shells to get a meal can get complicated but most of the time they will just simply hammer with their bills at the sides of shells to crack them open. Oystercatchers remain paired, keep the same mate year- around. They stay together, giving their pleasant whistling calls. They are committed to keeping a close, loving relationship. God made them that way for their good and so they can raise new families of Oystercatchers.

"Do not love the world or anything in the world. If anyone loves the world – the lust of the flesh, the lust of the eyes, and the pride of life – comes not from the Father but from the world."
1 John 2: 15-16

This scripture is very challenging in today's world. When we lust after something, we are wanting to choose ungodly behavior, ungodly words, words that hurt or ungodly lifestyles that separate us from God and from each other. Pornography is ungodly behavior and can lead to divorce and broken families. Ungodly behavior separates us from God and is often the reason for murders, drug addiction, alcoholism, child abuse and all for very selfish reasons. If you are feeling sad about some unpleasant memories because of your past then be very aware that Jesus went to the Cross for you and everyone's sin and you can be forgiven and restored back into God's presence by his grace. This grace means that we can do the next right thing if we will listen to God in his word and ignore what the world says to do! We are overcomers in Jesus Christ whose blood, sinless blood, was shed for all. Receive his love today and live for him the rest of your life. His love is eternal. He rose from the grave so you can live with him in glory.

Prayer: Lord God, thank you for the Cross, for shedding your sinless blood so I can live a life of freedom that comes from being forgiven. Help me to live for you and not for the world. Help me to be a living example of your grace at work in my life so many will want a relationship with you and believe your word for their salvation. I love you, Jesus, and want to tell others about this grace that gives me a new life; you call me "a new creation, a child of God." I am so happy that I want to sing like the Oystercatchers who stay together. In your precious name, the name of Jesus, and to bring you all the glory you so deserve, Amen.

Has you ever been overwhelmed by the beauty of one of God's creatures? This one may do that because it has familiar, warm colors, the top of a beautiful budded pine and also, the Bluebird is standing so still on such a narrow perch. He looks like he wants to linger a while, looking out over the forest, giving praise to God for this wonderful morning in the wild. He has no needs except looking for a few berries later. Could he be meditating? If so, on what? Is he aware of the photographer near-by? Probably not! "Billy Blue" is very contented, this will be only one of his many stops along his journey today. He will find food, he will take a nap, he will "sing when the spirit says sing." He may find his mate and they will dance and enjoy this day together; their way of starting a new family is building a nest, laying Bluebird eggs and then sit on them until they hatch. Does this remind you of the movie, "It's a Wonderful Life"? Not so much, because that was about humans and we are delving into the life of a Mountain bluebird. "Billy Blue" is just one of trillions of examples of life in this beautiful forest and beyond. What is God, our Lord, saying to us as we enjoy this marvelous bluebird he created?

"This is what the Lord says, He who made the earth, the Lord who formed it and established it – The Lord is his name: 'Call to me and I will answer you and tell you great and unsearchable things you do not know.'"
Jeremiah 33: 2-3

When we call out to God, the Lord, we are starting a loving relationship with him. He hears every voice that calls out to him because he first loved us so that we can love him and love other people. His love is called agape love. This kind of love is forgiving love just as if we never sinned. When we say 'yes Lord, I need you in my life,' He says, 'I have been waiting for you to call out to me. I am so glad that now I can call you a child of God. Please call out to me many times every day because I have great and unsearchable things you do not know.'"

"What a loving God, our Lord is! He went to the cross and did what his heavenly Father told him to do! His Father's orders: 'suffer this agonizing beating, this hatred for God and Godly living because of the sin of all people. Not one is righteous not one! You, Jesus, are the sacrificial Lamb for this sinful world.' A sinless God died on an old rugged cross. Never forget that we put him on the cross because of our sin! He forgives our sin and only asks us to: **"Love the Lord, your God, with all your heart and with all your soul and with all your mind and with all your strength, and neighbor as yourself." Mark 12: 30.** Let's call on him in prayer now:

Prayer: Lord God, Precious Lamb of God, who takes away the sins of the world, help me to live for you every day until You bring me home. I want to receive your agape love into my heart daily forever and ever. I love your word and want to read and memorize it to share with others. Holy Spirit, fill me and guide me, change me and use me, in Jesus' name, Amen.

Nothing but the Blood

1. What can wash a - way my sin? Noth - ing but the blood of
2. For my par - don this I see: noth - ing but the blood of
3. Noth - ing can for sin a - tone: noth - ing but the blood of
4. This is all my hope and peace: noth - ing but the blood of

Je - sus. What can make me whole a - gain?
Je - sus. For my clean - sing this my plea:
Je - sus. Naught of good that I have done:
Je - sus. This is all my right - eous - ness:

Refrain

Noth - ing but the blood of Je - sus.
noth - ing but the blood of Je - sus.
noth - ing but the blood of Je - sus.
noth - ing but the blood of Je - sus.

O pre - cious

is the flow that makes me white as snow; no o - ther

fount I know; noth - ing but the blood of Je - sus.

Text: Robert Lowry, 1876
Tune: Robert Lowry, 1876

78 78 Refrain
PLAINFIELD
www.hymnary.org/text/what_can_wash_away_my_sin

There Is a Balm in Gilead

Capo 3:

Refrain:
There is a balm in Gil-e-ad to make the wound-ed whole,
there is a balm in Gil-e-ad to heal the sin-sick soul.

1 Some times I feel dis-cour-aged and __ think my work's in vain,
2 If you can-not preach like Pe-ter, if you can-not pray like Paul,

but __ then the Ho-ly Spir-it re-vives my soul a-gain.
you can tell the love of Je-sus and say, "He died for all."

irregular
BALM IN GILEAD
www.hymnary.org/text/sometimes_i_feel_discouraged_spiritual

Text and tune: Afro-American spiritual

PART 3
"FAITH" HALL OF FAME

"Now faith is being sure of what we hope for and certain of what we do not see. This is what the ancients were commended for...... Hebrews 11:1

By faith we understand that the universe was formed at God's command, so that what is seen was not made out of what was visible.

By faith Able offered God, a better sacrifice than Cain did. By faith he was commended as a righteous man, when God spoke well of his offerings. And by faith he still speaks, even though he is dead.

By faith Enoch was taken from this life, so that he did not experience death; he could not be found, because God had taken him away. For before he was taken, he was commended as one who pleased God. And without faith it is impossible to please God, because anyone who comes to him must believe that he exists and that he rewards those who earnestly seek him.

By faith Noah, when warned about things not yet seen, in holy fear built an ark to save his family. By his faith he condemned the world and became heir of the righteousness that comes by faith.

By faith Abraham, when called to go to a place he would later receive as his inheritance, obeyed and went, even though he did not know where he was going. By faith he made his home in the promised land like a stranger in a foreign country; he lived in tents, as did Isaac and Jacob, who were heirs with him of the same promise. For he was looking forward to the city with foundations, whose architect and builder is God.

By faith Abraham, even though he was past age – and Sarah herself was barren – was enabled to become a father because he considered him faithful who had made the promise. And so, from this one man, and he as good as dead, came descendants as numerous as the stars in the sky and as countless as the sand on the seashore.

All these people were still living by faith when they died. They did not receive the things promised; they only saw them and welcomed them from a distance. And they admitted that they were aliens and strangers on earth. People who say such things show that they are looking for a country of their own. If they had been thinking of the country they had left, they would have had opportunity to return. Instead, they were looking for a better country – a heavenly one. Therefore, God is not ashamed to be called their God, for he has prepared a city for them.

By faith Abraham, when God tested him, offered Isaac as a sacrifice. He who has received the promise was about to sacrifice his one and only son, even though God had said to him, "It is through Isaac that your offspring will be reckoned." Abraham reasoned that God could raise the dead, and figuratively speaking, he did receive Isaac back from death.

By faith Isaac blessed Jacob and Esau in regard to their future. By faith Jacob, when he was dying, blessed each of Joseph's sons, and worshipped as he leaned on the top of his staff.

By faith Joseph, when his end was near, spoke about the exodus of the Israelites from Egypt and gave instructions about his bones.

By faith Moses' parents hid him for three months after he was born, because they say he was no ordinary child, and they were not afraid of the king's edict.

By faith Moses, when he has grown up, refused to be known as the son of Pharaoh's daughter. He chose to be mistreated along with the people of God rather to enjoy the pleasures of sin for a short time. He regarded disgrace for the sake of Christ as of greater value than the treasures of Egypt, because he was looking ahead to his reward. By faith he left Egypt, not fearing the king's anger; he persevered because he saw him who is invisible. By faith he kept the Passover and the sprinkling of blood, so the destroyer of the firstborn would not touch the firstborn of Israel.

By faith the people passed through the Red Sea as on dry land; but when the Egyptians tried to do so, they were drowned**.**

By faith the walls of Jericho fell, after the people had marched around them for seven days. By faith the prostitute Rahab, because she welcomed the spies, was not killed with those who were disobedient.

And what more shall I say? I do not have time to talk about Gideon, Barak, Samson, Jephthah, David, Samuel and the prophets, **who through faith** conquered kingdoms, administrated justice, and gained what was promised; who shut the mouths of lions, quenched the fury of the flames, and escaped the edge of the sword; whose weakness was turned to strength; and who became powerful in battle and routed foreign armies. Women received back their dead, raised to life again. Others were tortured and refused to be released, so that they might gain a better resurrection. Some faced jeers and flogging, while still others were chained and put in prison. They were stoned; they were sawed in two; they were put to death by the sword. They went about in sheepskins and goatskins, destitute, persecuted and mistreated – the world was not worthy of them. They wandered in deserts and mountains, and in caves and holes in the ground. **These were all commented for their faith,** yet none of them received what had been promised. God had planned something better for us so that only together with us would they be made perfect."

HEBREWS 11:2-40

May the God of peace, who through the blood of the eternal covenant brought back from the dead our Lord Jesus, that great Shepherd of the sheep, equip you with everything good for doing his will, and may he work in us what is pleasing to him, through Jesus Christ, to whom be glory for ever and ever, Amen.

HEBREWS 13:20-21

You may want to take a spotting scope with you when you go looking for a goldeneye, either Barrow's or Common goldeneye. Why? Well, the male Barrow's goldeneye has black and white feathers and his coloring is more like the Common loon. The female Barrow's goldeneye is this beautiful brown and white displayed in this photo. It sounds like the female is more colorful than the male which is rare in the bird world. They like small mountain lakes in the summer but then they move to inland rivers and lakes that are ice free. In winter and spring males gather around females to perform acrobatic courtship displays; but they are also known as a relatively quiet duck-like bird. However, during flights, the fast-moving wings create a low whistling sound.

There is a lake in Iceland where a small population of Barrow's goldeneye thrive because generations of "house duck" lovers, nickname given by the residents, are so happy with their community of fine feathered friends, the Barrow's goldeneye. In fact, the residents have created nest boxes for them on the sides of houses and barns. This is a source of pride for the generous property owners and must bring much joy as they watch them hatch, grow and change into responsible parents. This project also brings glory to God as he watches the love that is displayed when another nesting box is completed and another family moves in. This duck-like bird was named after Sir John Barrow and has a wingspan of 27-28 inches. The oldest know Barrow's goldeneye was a female that lived to at least 18 years old. A Mom and Dad goldeneye may separate during the summer months but they come back and find the same mate in the spring to start a new family. These diving birds forage underwater. They eat pond vegetation and aquatic insects; Like some of us humans, they like mussels as well.

Finally, all of you, live in harmony with one another; be sympathetic, love as brothers, be compassionate and humble. Do not repay evil with evil or insult with insult, but with blessing; because to this you were called so that you may inherit a blessing.
1 Peter 3: 8-9

Let's go back to that lake in Iceland where the Barrow's goldeneye thrive. Why do these birds thrive and survive so well? Could it be the love of the residents for these duck-like birds? Do they have something to be proud of because the birds come back year after year and find the same mate to start a new family? Do they cooperate with each other to be sure the goldeneyes are well provided for? Yes, to each question! What a blessing for the residents when the phones start ringing, "they are here! Let's go and see the blessings!"

Prayer: Lord God, thank you for the blessings you bring to this community as the birds return to nesting boxes and the beauty of all the people coming out to greet each other and welcome the flock home. Protect them every year and grow the faith of the people so that their churches are full of residents who love God and help care for these precious birds, in Jesus' name and to glorify the Cross of Christ, which makes all these blessings possible, Amen.

The Tricolored heron, formerly known as the Louisiana heron, is a small species of heron native to coastal parts of the Americas, in the Atlantic region. The Tricolored heron has more than three colors. "Multi – colored heron" might be a more accurate name for this small wading bird. Standing statue-still over the surface, a Tricolored heron will suddenly slash its head through the reeds, its bill spearing an unsuspected frog. Gobbling down its meal, the heron spreads its wings and flies to a new hunting location, revealing a flash of its white belly.

During mating season, they have more vibrant color changes. Their bills and facial skin take on a bright, cobalt blue and their yellow legs transform into pink. Why? These coloration infusions are all about attracting a mate. The President of the Tampa Audubon Society expresses a fond heart for these herons. "I love watching the baby birds as they grow up, being fed by their parents. I love the noise – the cacophony – it's an orchestra of so many different sounds from the adults and the chicks." Constructing the stick nest is part of their courtship ritual. The males supply the sticks while the females weave them into a platform with a wide depression in the middle.

"Come, let us bow down in worship, let us kneel before the Lord our Maker; for he is our God and we are the people of his pasture, the flock under his care. Today, if only you would hear his voice."
Psalm 95: 6-7

The Lord our Maker is also the Lord that made all of the wildlife in the world. He created this colorful and very interesting Tricolored heron. The flock of herons that the Audubon President loves to watch and listen to are a flock under God's care 24/7 as well as looking after you 24/7. God loves his creatures in his creation. If God loves these herons, then how much more does he love you; you who are made in the image of God? You, who hear his voice through this scripture and you, who pray now and listen to what God says back to you through the Holy Spirit. God is a very personal God and wants you to hear his voice day and night.

Prayer: Lord God, your love means so much to me and is available to me 24/7 and for the whole wide, wild world. Thank you for teaching me through these amazing herons that you deeply love all you have created. I want to hear your voice clearly every day from now on. Never stop talking to me because you have so much more love and wisdom that I need every single day. Someday, can I hear the orchestra of wild herons just like the Audubon President did? I hope so because I think it will be a lot of fun, in Jesus' name, Amen.

EASTERN BLUEBIRDS – *resting together*   Sialia sialis

Duanesburg, New York   Fairly common

The favorite Eastern bluebirds are increasing in numbers again, undoubtedly helped by birdhouses in many areas. Members of the Thrush family, they love open country with scattered trees, farms, and roadsides where they find bluebird houses that some caring farmer has placed in a convenient place for them to find. In the winter, they wonder to other habitats. They are blessed when they find bluebird trails, which means bluebird houses have been built in large quantities along trails that make life and growing new families very easy.

When they are not nesting, they can be found roaming the countryside in small flocks. One or two broods a year are found in some familiar species of birds but three broods a year are possible with Eastern bluebirds. The first brood may wind up feeding the second and third brood. When Dad is near, he may feed Mom and when Mom and Dad are close together they may preen each other's feathers. Preen means to get rid of unwanted, old feathers.

"Therefore, as God's chosen people, holy and dearly loved, clothe yourselves with compassion, kindness, humility, gentleness, and patience."
Colossians 3: 12

Can you identify the acts of compassion, kindness, and gentleness in Eastern bluebirds as you reread the second paragraph above? Amazing love is demonstrated in the way God created these precious bluebirds to help each other with their routine daily problems; And they sometimes have three broods of babies during one year. They keep busy but it is a labor of love because their kindness never stops or changes. God made them that way! Yes, we can always show God's love to others with the same actions. Who needs a little kindness in their life today? Is there someone who has suffered a loss or who is sick in the hospital? Let's ask God to help us find where we are needed today.

Prayer: Lord God, I are so grateful for your scriptures that help me live a holy life. Show me today the special person or family where I am needed to show God's amazing love and compassion. Prepare their hearts to receive your love as I go forth to share my time, bringing to them kindness, patience and humility. Do they need something I own? Do they need a hug? Can I help someone with a challenging project, or bring a meal to a sick or grieving Mom or help a Dad with painting his garage? Who can I pray with to help them through a very tough decision or the pain of an unwanted change? Thank you, Lord, for what you and I are going to do together to show Godly love, compassion, kindness and patience today, In Jesus' name, Amen.

BOBOLINK – *male singing in spring finery*   *Dolichonyx oryzivorus*

Canada   *In decline*

The Bobolink builds his nest on the ground with grass and twigs. The reason for the decline in their population is because the farmers often mow early in the spring and the nests are destroyed before the eggs hatch or just after they are hatched. The livestock graze on the ground and they are known to disrupt the nests and those baby chicks never make it to safety. The Bobolink migrates in cool weather to Argentina, Bolivia, Brazil, and Paraguay. How sad after that very long journey, they arrive in Canada with God's protection, only to lose their family because of the spring farming practices in Canada. The black and white feathers on his back are unique in that they look like a tuxedo on backwards. Notice the male's rich straw – colored patch on his head, along with his singing posture that produces a bubbling, virtuoso song. An old-fashioned name for this bird is, "Rice Bird" for his tendency to feed on cultivated grains. As summer ends, he molts into a buff and brown female-like plumage. Can we do anything to help the Bobolinks survive the farmers mowing and the livestock chewing?

"If you come across a bird's nest beside the road, either in a tree or on the ground, and the mother is sitting on the eggs, do not take the mother with the young; You may take the young but be sure to let the mother go, so that it may go well with you and you may have a long life."
Deuteronomy 22: 6 -7

How amazing is this! God has an answer for saving these babies and making sure that life goes well for us, His children. We can take these eggs or newborns home and help them grow to be healthy Bobolinks. Who knew? GOD KNOWS! Are you surprised that God knows all about every nest and every bird that needs protecting? Are you surprised that the mother should not be harmed or captured? Shouldn't she stay with the babies? What is God's plan? Could it be that Mom Bobolink, if left in the meadow area, may be able to have another family there that will survive the next time? By helping the babies get strong and go back to the meadow then they can have families of their own! God loves you so much more than He loves His birds! He made you, His child, in His image! We can not be God, but if we love God, we can grow to be like Him! Let's pray with a thankful heart:

Prayer: Lord God, Creator of everything good, especially these very special Bobolinks and their families. I want to know how I can help save your endangered birds in the wild. I love them because of their eye-catching colors and their beautiful singing. I am so thankful for my life with you, Lord, and the life in nature that has so much variety and purpose. I am wanting more of you in my life, God, and through nature I am learning how much more you love me than I ever thought possible. The Cross and your blood shed for me makes all this possible and it is hard to find words to tell you how you much your unconditional love means to me. My heart of praise is my offering to you this morning, in Jesus precious name, Amen.

This proud looking, crested bird is royal blue and black in color. The photographer agreed to use a nickname for him to help us identify him in the wild. So, even though this jay was named after a man named Steller, we will sometimes refer to him as "Mr. Royal blue and black." There are 18 subspecies of Steller's jay, ranging from Alaska to Nicaragua, with nine found north of Mexico. The Steller's jay is also known as Long-crested jay, Mountain jay and Pine jay. God created many jays because he loves them and wants us to appreciate their beauty as well. They are not always doing good things but you have to admit they are colorful. The fact is that these jays have been seen attacking and killing small birds like the Pygmy nuthatch and the Dark-eyed junco.

Steller's jays were discovered on an Alaskan Island in 1741 by George Steller, a naturalist on a Russian explorer's ship. At that time and around 1788, there were other discoveries that also were credited to Mr. Steller. So, now when birding in Alaska, we can also look for Steller's sea-lions and Steller's sea-eagles.

The Lord will keep you from all harm – he will watch over your life; The Lord will watch over your coming and going both now and forevermore.
Psalm 121: 7-8

The oldest Steller's jay or "Mr. Royal blue and black" was a male and at least 16 years, one month old when he was found in Alaska in 1987. He was originally banded there in 1972. Does this survival rate amaze you? Yes, God's survival rate for his creatures and his children are nothing short of miraculous! Think of all the wind, rain and snowstorms this jay and his family have encountered and survived! Every day is a gift, every breath is more precious than gold or silver. Do you agree? Can we spend a few moments now in praise and thanksgiving for God's goodness to us and to Mr. Royal blue and black? God has given all of his creation life; God lovers, nature lovers, jays, woodpeckers, sparrows, apple trees, roses, all live because God gives them life. **Psalm 121: 7-8** is a great promise from God to put on your memory list and share it with your friends when they are listening and need encouragement.

Prayer: Lord God, who not only gives abundant life but also gives me daily protection from harm, sees me every day whether I am out on the run or inside reading the Bible, or this Devotional Book Inspired by Nature or a sports magazine. Your love for me, Lord, is always with me, always watching over all I do, all I say and your promise is forevermore. I love you, Lord, and thank you for all the variety in nature and all the different people groups you created all over the world. I hope they all know this promise in Psalm 121: 7-8 that you love them and watch over them every day and forevermore, in Jesus' name, Amen.

RED – NAPED SAPSUCKER – *sipping sap*   *Sphyrapicus nuchalis*

British Columbia, Canada   *Uncommon*

....

The Red-naped sapsucker is a medium-sized North American woodpecker. Long thought to be a subspecies of the Yellow-bellied sapsucker. There are also white-naped, golden-naped golden-fronted, golden olive and grey-headed woodpeckers. Sapsuckers are industrious woodpeckers with a taste for sugar. They drill neat little rows of holes in trees. They like to drill in aspen, birch, and willow trees to lap up the sugary sap that flows out. The presence of sap wells is a good indication that they are around; but, so are their harsh wailing cries and stuttered drumming. The red patch on the back of their head helps separate these sharply dressed black and white sapsuckers from Yellow - bellied sapsuckers in the East and the Red- breasted sapsuckers along the Western coastal states.

Sapsuckers, despite what their name implies, do not suck sap, but are specialized for sipping it. Their tongues are shorter than other woodpeckers, and do not extend as far out. They lap sap up with the tip of their tongue, which has small hairlike projections that help hold the sap, much like a paintbrush holds paint. The oldest recorded Red-naped sapsucker was at least 4 years, 11 months old when she was found in Wyoming in 2011, the same state where she had been banded in 2008.

"Accept one another, then, just as Christ accepted you, in order to bring praise to God."
Romans 15: 7

While researching this woodpecker/sapsucker photo there was much ambiguity . Even the spell checker on the computer got confused. The solution may be that among the specie of woodpecker there are a few sapsuckers that have almost the same habits but the few differences cause them to have a different lifestyle. Please don't get off the rails here; God is not confused. This scripture tells us that birds and people have somethings in common and somethings very different in lifestyles and abilities. God does not make mistakes, we do! The way to glorify God with praise is to look for the best qualities in humans and in nature and thank God for all the good he has created. Show people love and acceptance because Jesus Christ loves and accepts everyone and all he has created in nature. It is sin that separates us from God and others. The Cross of Calvary changes everything when we accept Jesus and his blood shed on the cross for the forgiveness of sin.

Prayer: Lord God, thank you for reminding us that even though you created different skin colors, different hair, different abilities, your love for us never fails and we can love and accept everyone just as you showed us on the cross. Help us tell the world that you, Jesus, died for all so we can be forgiven and accept all of creation just as you have done. Woodpeckers do not need forgiveness but we do. Sin separates us from you but the cross brings us together to love and accept one another. All praise and glory to you, King of Kings and Lord of Lords, in the precious name of Jesus, the name above all names, Amen.

One of the most abundant birds across North America, and one of the most boldly colored, the Red-winged blackbird is a familiar sight atop cattails, along soggy roadsides and on telephone wires. Glossy black males have scarlet and yellow shoulder patches. They can puff up or hide these patches depending on how confident they feel. The female looks like a large, dark sparrow. To attract them to your yard, you might try spreading grain on the ground rather than a feeder on a pole. They are ground foragers and find insects there when they are hungry. The male Red-winged black bird spends a lot of time defending his territory during mating season. He chases other males out of his territory and attacks nest predators, sometimes going after larger animals, including horses and people. These colorful birds are so exciting when in flight. Those scarlet and yellow markings are brilliant and so spectacular when seen up close. This author loves these yearly spring friends because they love our property out in the country and so many fly over and back all day long.

"Shout for joy to the Lord, all the earth. Worship the Lord with gladness; come before him with joyful songs. Know that the Lord is God. It is he who made us, and we are his; we are his people, the sheep of his pasture. Enter his gates with thanksgiving and his courts with praise; give thanks to him and praise his name. For the Lord is good and his love endures forever; his faithfulness continues through all generations."

Psalm 100

When the Red-winged blackbirds fly overhead and swirl around the yard, over the barn and back to the house, I sit and marvel at the beauty not only in the colors displayed in Red-winged blackbirds but also the joy they bring to the ears. The song they sing expresses their joy and the love they have for life. The Red-winged blackbird's great beauty and their endearing song is how God created them, proving that his (God's) faithfulness continues through all generations. Do you have favorite birds that you look forward to every year as they return to your location? What are the reasons that you want to see them again? Do you feed them and take photos of them? Why? It is time to thank God for his wonderful, beautiful, musical and wild avian kingdom.

Prayer: Lord God, thank you so much for the variety in the avian kingdom. The colors are spectacular and the music from the songbirds is so joyful and full of life. We can never know how you created so many interesting living things for us to enjoy. But we are so happy and blessed that we get to enjoy so much of your creation in our life however long we live. To say you are faithful and generous is an understatement! You give Life, Love and Happiness to all who trust you and worship and praise your holy name, in the love of Christ, our Blessed Hope, who created the Red-winged blackbirds and the one who is coming back to earth to rule and reign forever, Amen.

FULL MOON OVER WARM ALASKAN SUNSET

"The Beauty and Warmth of God's Love" – Faith For An Upside-down World - 2022

FAITHFUL FLOCK FLYING SOUTH SINGING GOD'S LOVE SONGS

If you have read the last few pages of Volume 4, "DIVINE LOVE, " then you will recognize this photo but with something new; a flock of geese heading south for the winter. They are doing exactly what God planned for them from the beginning of the avian kingdom, starting in the garden of Eden. God is glorified in this photo for being the Creator of all life as this flock of feathered friends fly forward together into southern sunshine. The geese are migrating south for the winter in a close formation, just exactly how God planned their life from the beginning of time. God is faithful to all of his creation. God's people have been given "free will" but these faithful geese have been given Godly instinct to do the next right thing. Following these God given plans brings God glory.

In order for humans to give God glory, we need to accept **Jesus Christ** as our Savior because of what he did on the Cross; the sinless Son of God crucified by evil men so we can be forgiven of our sins. This is the **Beauty and Warmth of God's love** in action. Those who surrender to the Son of God have a personal relationship with Him through the Holy Spirit given at conversion. **John Wesley, in his book, "My Heart Was Strangely Warmed" calls this " Regeneration; A new life in Christ."** Also, God asks us to be Holy as he is Holy and when we miss the mark, we ask God for forgiveness and a restart is given.

If we confess our sins, he is faithful and just and will forgive us our sins and purify us from all unrighteousness. 1 John 1: 9. This restart is the **Beauty and Warmth of God's love** to continue living a righteous life in Christ as His child. You may agree or not; but studying about God in Nature is incredibly interesting and very enlightening at any age. **The Beauty and Warmth of God's love** is beyond human description. God's love is freedom to live for him and bring him glory now and for eternity. We are called to be faithful and do the next right thing, just like the geese!

"Now I am going to him who sent me, yet none of you asks me, 'Where are you going? Because I have said these things, you are filled with grief. But I tell you the truth: It is for your good that I am going away. Unless I go away, the Counselor will not come to you; but if I go, I will send him to you. When he comes, he will convict the world of guilt in regard to sin, righteousness and judgement. In regard to sin, because men do not believe in me; in regard to righteousness, because I am going to the Father, where you can see me no longer; in regard to judgement, because the prince of this world (Satan) now stands condemned. I have told you these things, so that in me you may have peace. In this world you will have trouble, But take heart! I have overcome the world.' " John 16: 5-11, 33.

Prayer: Merciful and Grace-filled God, my Lord and Savior, I am unworthy of the Beauty and Warmth of your love but your love abounds way beyond all boundaries and I am so grateful for PENTECOST! I need you more than ever and I know you are listening and that your love never fails. You, Lord God, are worthy of all my praise as I lift Holy Hands toward heaven. Thank you for your blood shed for me on the Cross. I am experiencing more and more the peace that passes all understanding; the joy of the Lord, which is my strength and the unconditional love of Jesus, the Son of God, who has saved me and is interceding for me in heaven as promised, in Jesus' precious name and to glorify Father, Son and Holy Spirit throughout all eternity, Amen.

PRAYER

Daily prayer of confession is a noble goal for Christians but not always the path we choose first thing in the morning or the last thing before falling asleep at night. It is a given that most Christians pray many times through out the day and sometimes in the night. We choose this because God is Sovern over all situations, whether good or bad, over all believers, young in the faith, or warriors in the faith. Try starting your day with a short prayer like: 'Lord, teach me today to stay in a prayerful attitude and pray with a sincere heart, in Jesus name, Amen.' At the end of the day, 'Thank you, Lord, for Your patient love and gracious guidance today in Jesus name, Amen.'

THE LORD'S PRAYER

Our Father, who art in heaven, hallowed be Thy name.
Thy kingdom come, Thy will be done on earth as it is in heaven.
Give us this day our daily bread, and forgive our trespasses,
As we forgive those who trespass against us.
And lead us not into temptation, but deliver us from evil.
For Thine is the kingdom, and the power, and the glory, forever, Amen.

(1989- United Methodist Hymnal - #895)

HOW TO PRAY

Lord, I am no longer my own, but Yours. Put me to what
You will, rank me with who You will.

Let me be employed by You or laid aside for You, exalted for You, or brought low for You.

Let me have all things, let me have nothing, I freely and heartily
yield all things to Your pleasure and disposal.

And now, O glorious and blessed God, Father, Son, and Holy Spirit,

You are mine and I am Yours. So be it. Amen.

THE BEST OF JOHN WESLEY ON PRAYER – (2007 - Barbour Publishing, Inc.)

PRAYER OF CONFESSION

O God, I confess the blindness that is not aware of sinning; the pride that dares

not admit that it is wrong; the selfishness that can see nothing but its own will;

the righteousness that knows no fault; the callousness that has ceased to care;

the defiance that does not regret its own sin; the evasion that always tries

to make excuses;

the coldness of heart that is too hardened to repent; God, I am a sinner;

be merciful to me.

Give me at all times, eyes which are open to my own faults; a conscience which is sensitive and quick to warn; a heart that cannot sin in peace; but is moved to regret and remorse.

So, grant that being truly penitent, I may be truly forgiven; so that I may find that your love is great enough to cover my sin; through Jesus Christ, my Lord,

Amen.

William Barclay in "Prayer for the Christian Year," – 1965, abebooks.com

SIGNS of The END of The AGE

"Immediately after the distress of those days, the sun will be darkened, and the moon will not give its light; the stars will fall from the sky, and the heavenly bodies will be shaken. At that time the sign of the Son of Man will appear in the sky, and all the nations of the earth will mourn. They will see the Son of Man coming on the clouds of the sky, with power and great glory. And he will send his angels with a loud trumpet call, and they will gather his elect from the four winds, from one end to the other."

"No one knows about that day or hour, not even the Son, but only the Father."

MATTHEW 24:29-31,36

FALSE TEACHERS – Heed Biblical Warnings

JUDE

Introduction:

Jude, like James, was a brother of Jesus. He wrote to warn Christians about the same false teachers Peter wrote about in his second letter. These false teachers were not only teaching that Jesus was not the Son of God, they were also leading the people to live sinful lives. Jude warns that God will punish and destroy these false teachers just as he had punished sinners in the Old Testament.

Introduction (1,2) Warnings against false teachers (3-16) Warning and conclusion (17 – 25)

Jude, a servant of Jesus Christ and a brother of James, to those who have been called, who are loved by God the Father and kept by Jesus Christ: Mercy, peace and love be yours in abundance.

The Sin and Doom of Godless Men

"Dear Friends, although I was very eager to write to you about the salvation we share, I felt I had to write and urge you to contend for the faith that was once for all entrusted to the saints. For certain men whose condemnation was written about long ago have secretly slipped in among you. They are godless men, who change the grace of our God into license for immorality and deny Jesus Christ our only Sovereign and Lord.

Though you already know all this, I want to remind you that the Lord delivered his people out of Egypt, but later destroyed those who did not believe. And the angels that did not keep their positions of authority but abandoned their own homes – these he has kept in darkness, abound with everlasting chains for judgement on the great Day. In a similar way, Sodom and Gomorrah and the surrounding towns gave themselves up to sexual immorality and perversion. They serve as an example of those who suffer the punishment of eternal fire.

In the very same way, these dreamers pollute their own bodies, reject authority and slander celestial beings. But even the archangel Michael, when he was disputing with the devil about the body of Moses, did not dare to bring a slanderous accusation against him, but said, 'The Lord rebuke you!' Yet these men speak abusively against whatever they do not understand; and what things they do understand by instinct, like unreasoning animals – these are the very things that destroy them.

Woe to them! They have taken the way of Cain; they have rushed for profit into Balaam's error; they have been destroyed in Korah's rebellion.

These men are blemishes at your love feasts, eating with you without the slightest qualm – shepherds who feed only themselves. They are clouds without rain, blown along by the wind; autumn trees without fruit and uprooted – twice dead. They are wild waves of the sea, foaming up their shame; wandering stars, for whom blackest darkness has been reserved forever.

Enoch, the seventh from Adam, prophesied about these men: 'See the Lord is coming with thousands upon thousands of his holy ones to judge everyone, and to convict all the ungodly acts they have done in the ungodly way, and of all the harsh words ungodly sinners have spoken against him. These men are grumblers and faultfinders; they follow their own evil desires; they boast about themselves and flatter others for their own advantage.'"

A Call to Persevere

"But, dear friends, remember what the apostles of our Lord Jesus Christ foretold. They said to you, 'In the last times there will be scoffers who will follow their own ungodly desires. These are the men who divide you, who follow mere natural instincts and do not have the Spirit.'

But you dear friends, 'build yourselves up in the most holy faith and pray in the Holy Spirit. Keep yourselves in God's love as you wait for the mercy of our Lord Jesus Christ to bring you to eternal life.

Be merciful to those who doubt; snatch others from the fire and save them; to others show mercy, mixed with fear – hating even the clothing stained by corrupted flesh.'"

DOXOLOGY

"To him who is able to keep you from falling and to present you before his glorious presence without fault and with great joy – to the only God our Savior be glory, majesty, power and authority, through Jesus Christ our Lord, before all ages, now and forevermore! Amen." JUDE 1 – 25

False Teachers and Their Destruction

Selected Scriptures from **2 Peter 1 – 14**

"But there were also false prophets among the people, just as there will be false teachers among you. They will secretly introduce destructive heresies, even denying the Sovereign Lord who bought them – bringing swift destruction on themselves. Many will follow their shameful ways and will bring the way of truth into disrepute." **2 Peter: 1 - 4**

"They will be paid back with harm for the harm they have done. Their idea of pleasure is to carouse in broad daylight. They are blots and blemishes, reveling in their pleasures while they feast with you. With eyes full of adultery, they never stop sinning; they seduce the unstable; they are experts in greed – an accursed brood!" **2 Peter: 13 -14**

Blessed Assurance

Text: Fanny J. Crosby (1820-1915)
Tune: Phoebe P. Knapp (1839-1908)

9 10 99 Refrain
ASSURANCE
www.hymnary.org/text/blessed_assurance_jesus_is_mine

Take My Life and Let It Be

1 Take my life and let it be con-se-crat-ed, Lord, to thee. Take my mo-ments and my days; let them flow in end-less praise, let them flow in end-less praise.

2 Take my hands and let them move at the im-pulse of thy love. Take my feet and let them be swift and beau-ti-ful for thee, swift and beau-ti-ful for thee.

3 Take my voice and let me sing al-ways, on-ly, for my King. Take my lips and let them be filled with mes-sag-es from thee, filled with mes-sag-es from thee.

4 Take my sil-ver and my gold; not a mite would I with-hold. Take my in-tel-lect and use ev-ery power as thou shalt choose, ev-ery power as thou shalt choose.

5 Take my will and make it thine;
it shall be no longer mine.
Take my heart—it is thine own;
it shall be thy royal throne,
it shall be thy royal throne.

6 Take my love; my Lord, I pour
at thy feet its treasure store.
Take myself, and I will be
ever, only, all for thee,
ever, only, all for thee.

Text: Frances R. Havergal, 1874
Tune: H. A. Cesar Malan, 1827

77 77 with repeat
HENDON
www.hymnary.org/text/take_my_life_and_let_it_be

PERSONAL TESTIMONY OF THE BAPTISM IN THE HOLY SPIRIT WITH EVIDENCE OF TONGUES

by Shirley D. Andrews

In the year 1978 on February 11, this author was "Born Again" with the knowledge that I had received salvation and the Holy Spirit; Christ alive in me my hope of glory; also, was justified (just as if I never sinned) and also had minimally started the sanctification that comes with a surrendered heart to Jesus Christ and Him crucified. I knew a change had taken place but the totality of that change was not revealed until the joy began to flow in my heart and I hope outward to those around me; that joy continues to this very day in 2022.

It happened during an altar call at a Methodist church in Saratoga County, in N.Y. The occasion was a Lay Witness Mission which started on Friday at dinner in the Fellowship Hall and ended at the altar during Sunday morning worship. The Methodist evangelist for this event had traveled from California to lead this life changing weekend. He had called his team, families from all over the Northeast, to come to this church to bear witness to the life changing power of Jesus Christ and Him crucified for the sins of the world. My family, husband, daughter and son all agreed to do this as my husband and I had agreed to do the planning and carrying out of a Friday night dinner for all the guests that would be coming from out of town as witnesses for Jesus Christ. We all had amazing experiences that we shared at the Sunday evening evaluation meeting back in Fellowship Hall. And much to my surprise, we all had signed "yes" on the card to going out to be witnesses for Jesus. We did that for a few years, three or four, until the scheduling got too complicated. One February vacation from school took us to San Jose, CA Methodist church to tell those folks about how God got our attention about our sin and His righteousness and forgiveness for sin. God was changing how we think about life, heaven, hell and especially about our daily relationship with God.

Now, fast forward to the year 2000, my husband is diagnosed with cancer and five months later is with the Lord. I was now in the Free Methodist church because they offered the Bible studies I was craving for. I have never stopped reading and learning about God's word. Next, my friends invite me to a Joyce Meyer Conference in Worchester, MA and at the end, after the TV cameras were off, Joyce asked if anyone wanted to be Baptized in the Holy Spirit with the evidence of speaking in any other tongue.

We had an "Assembly of God" friend on this trip with us from Corinth, N.Y. and we had been to a couple of her worship services and, of course, both Johanna and I raised our hands. We both wanted more of God and His power in our lives. Our Pentecostal friend was directed by Joyce to lay on hands of those with their hands raised. Joyce prayed a general prayer for God to impart a new tongue and that is exactly what happened. Both Johanna and I started speaking in "tongues" at the same time but both a different and unrecognizable language. We were told that this was the next step to service for God as Joyce explained it to us. We were very surprised that this happened to us but we are forever grateful to God for anointing us in this language that is spoken somewhere in the world; neither of us knows where this language is spoken but we are both very sure that it was from Jesus to bless us. We have been told that not only do we have this prayer language as a prophetic gift but also to build up our own Spiritual fitness when we feel the need to get closer and closer to God. I have been in services that have had a prophetic tongue speak out and another person to give the Interpretation. All this is very real and very beneficial to all who believe! Seek all of God, He wants to bless you! **Joy, Peace and Love in Christ, Shirley D. Andrews.**

PHOTOGRAPHER
J. Michael Fuller

Mike holds bachelor and master's degrees from Albany State University in Albany, NY. He spent 28 years as a 5th and 6th grade teacher, specializing in science. Many students in the Scotia-Glenville School district Scotia, NY benefitted from Mike's expertise in teaching about the world around us, above us and beyond. He passed on to his students a love for learning, and a respect for God's creation, Mike and his wife also taught Sunday school for many years before she passed away several years ago.

In retirement, Mike continues his life-long passion for photography. He has been published on "Ranger Rick" and "Audubon" covers, Sierra Club and Audubon Society calendars and published in "International wildlife" and other publications. He travels extensively in pursuit of new close-up shots of God's magnificent creatures. He lives in Duanesburg, NY on his 42 acres with ponds, woods and hills to climb. His woods are full of songbirds, maybe because he has delicious bird feeders scattered strategically around his quiet property.

AUTHOR
Shirley D. Andrews

Shirley is a graduate of Eastman School of Music in Rochester, NY and has a masters degree from the Crane School of Music in Potsdam, NY. She taught elementary public school music for 31 years. Most of those years were in the Scotia-Glenville School District. She also taught music education classes at Schenectady County Community College. She loved her career in teaching and Music Ministry. She has two children and two grandchildren.

After retirement and the death of her husband, Shirley pursued a career as a Certified Lay Minister in the Upper New York Annual Conference, Adirondack District of the U M Church. She has had leadership positions at Porter's Corners UMC, Ballston Spa UMC, and led worship at Woodlawn Commons in the Wesley Community.

Shirley continues to be passionate about Devotional writing Inspired by Nature for God lovers, God seekers, nature lovers, and the Family Altar. A future project might be "ON THE ROAD TO DAMASCUS" A Devotional inspired by the Nature: Volume 6, exploring the life and ministry of the Apostle Paul. Samples of Shirley's first 4 Devotionals can be seen on her website www.shirleydandrews.com.

REFERENCES

Book of North American Birds, The Reader's Digest Association, Inc. Pleasantville, NY/Montreal - 1990

Peterson Field Guide to Birds of Eastern and Central North America, by Roger Tory Peterson; text copyright 2010 by the Marital Trust B - sixth edition

National Audubon Society Field Guide to North American Birds - Eastern Region; copyright 1994 by Chanticleer Press, Inc. - second edition

www.allaboutbirds.com

www.birds.cornell.edu

www.nationalgeographics.com/mammals/animals

Oxford Dictionary, published, created and produced in the United States and Great Britain in 1998 by Dorling Kindersley Limited and Oxford University Press, Inc.

www.wikipedia.com - North American wildlife in wilderness areas

www.alaskanwildlife.org

Holy Bible - NIV - Copyright 1990 - Zondervan Publishing House, Grand Rapids, Michigan - second edition

Zondervan Exhaustive Concordance - NIV - 1999, Zondervan Publishing House, Grand Rapids, Michigan - second edition

www.hymnary.org

The Best of Birds and Blooms Book, 2022

NAMES of THE HOLY SPIRIT - ROSE PUBLISHING, Peabody MA, www.HendricksonRose.com

Printed in the United States
by Baker & Taylor Publisher Services